Jack
Cassady's
the
Best of Monday
Funnies & MORE

Jack Cassady's
the Best of **Monday**
Funnies & MORE

To Daine & Tom
with Best wishes!
Keep smiling!

Jack Cassady

John R. "Jack" Cassady

Cartoonist's Disclaimer
All characters in this book are either fictitious or not. While some events actually occurred, others did not. Any resemblance to real persons, living, dead or undead, is mostly coincidental…

To order additional copies of this book, contact:
Xlibris Corporation
1-888-795-4274
www.Xlibris.com
Orders@Xlibris.com

*This book is dedicated to my family, friends, veterans
and fans of cartoon art everywhere…*

FORWARD

Jack Cassady has a long history of making life more fun for everyone. In fact, he's devoted his life to it. With his humorous writing and drawing he has been devoted to starting everyone's week off with a smile. His feature, Monday's Funnies got the job done. It's what the world needs more of, and now he has a collection of his laughs over the years in book form so we can keep smiling forever.

As a professional cartoon humorist I know how hard it is to create good humor on a regular schedule so his efforts fill me with admiration as I laugh. I know personally how valuable this talent is and I hope Jack can keep it up so future generations can enjoy a life of good cheer.

INTRODUCTION

The purpose of this book is to entertain and amuse readers with cartoons and text from my internet/email weekly feature along with cartoons and writings not seen before. "The Monday Funnies" feature started years ago as a light-hearted effort to help folks start their work-week with a smile or laugh. Humor is good medicine (a' la Dr. Patch Adams) and a decent defense against insanity. In a world of instant communications, bad news, wars, hatred, fear, stress and uncertainty, it's a prescription offering temporary relief and enjoyment for those able to invest a little time and have some fun.

My earliest recollection of the power of visual art and humor happened when I was about four years old. I discovered my drawings, which gave me pleasure, attracted attention and entertained others. That discovery was reinforced by the enjoyment my Mother expressed as she happily read magazine and newspaper cartoons. As a youngster, I sat at her knee and thought how nice it would be to be able to delight readers with funny drawings. From those early days cartooning became a part of my life. Now it's part of my personality. When I'm not drawing or doodling, I'm thinking or writing about it.

Growing up in a single parent household, I spent much time alone. I was a charter member of the "Latchkey Kids" club. My imagination was put to good use through much drawing. I created imaginary worlds, people, creatures, critters and friends. After all these years, I still love it now as much as when I started. I agree with the late great cartoonist Dik Browne creator of "Hagar the Horrible". Dik said "Cartooning is such a pleasant way of making a living. I would love to do it, if God doesn't mind, for eternity." To me, it doesn't get much better than that.

Another lifetime affection of mine is our Armed Forces, specifically the U.S. Army and the U.S. Marine Corps. I had the honor and privilege of serving our nation as an officer in the U.S. Army for twenty-two years. Two of those years were in combat duty with the Army's Green Berets in Vietnam and Laos. I feel close to the special operations community and am especially proud of having served with some of our country's finest warriors. My connection with the Marines was inherited from my father. He was a career Non-Commissioned Officer and veteran of the First Marine Division in the Pacific in WW II and later the Korean War. Dad's respect and "Semper Fi" pride in the Corps rubbed off on me.

I've been influenced by great numbers of artists, professors, writers and cartoonists. Most are sharp witted, warm, intelligent and multi-talented creators who are fun to be around. Some cartoonists, like Beetle Baily's Mort Walker, have influenced me beyond their realizations. I appreciate them, what they do and their support. To those who subscribe to Cassady's MONDAY FUNNIES internet/email feature, **Thanks, enjoy and keep smiling!**

www.ToonMaker.com

CONTENTS

CHAPTER I.

FROM THE EDGE OF THE GRID...
(general humor from daily life, business, sports, etc.)

"Cartoonists and humorists always
sit at the children's table."

Jack Cassady with thanks to Woody Allen

"It's not cave art. It's an app for my smart phone."

"This lovely piece comes with a full
maintenance agreement and tech support."

JOHN R. "JACK" CASSADY

"When are they coming out on kindle or nook?"

"Now do you believe in illegal aliens?"

JOHN R. "JACK" CASSADY

"I'm in a great mood today. The NASDAQ is up 20 points and I'm down 10 lbs."

"When I was your age, I had to kayak to school."

"If we're 'going for broke', we're a success."

"When he takes up a hobby, he really goes <u>all the way</u>!"

"Of course I'll tell you the meaning of life, if
you give me twenty bucks of it first."

"How did things go at school today?"

JOHN R. "JACK" CASSADY

"Who owns the mineral rights to this meal?"

"…But I still have projects to finish!"

"Here's our chance. Invite everybody we owe over for dinner!"

"I've enrolled in a self-improvement course.
I'm leaving you."

JOHN R. "JACK" CASSADY

"It appears that money wasn't the root of all evil after all."

"I had a pretty good public school education but
I don't know anything about prayer or
evolution."

"I think we're way ahead of this cashless Society thing."

"They're much more organized this year."

JOHN R. "JACK" CASSADY

"Staying within our budget is easy. Don't buy anything."

JOHN R. "JACK" CASSADY

"That's really all you need to know how to do.
You'll be working nights at the quick shop at the
corner of …"

"I found a simple way of balancing our budget.
I sold the planes."

JOHN R. "JACK" CASSADY

"Tell Brutus I'm booked solid. Give him an
appointment for the Ides of March."

"We're really looking for someone with a more
direct genealogical connection to the boss."

JOHN R. "JACK" CASSADY

"I see your team in the playoffs…"

"We got group rates."

"He is an Officer and Gentleman, just not at the same time."

JOHN R. "JACK" CASSADY

"When you gotta go, you gotta go, and YOU gotta go!"

Paratrooper's jump run…

"I understand you asked for a lawyer. You're in luck. We've got lots of them…"

"...and give up jogging!"

"I had a difficult delivery too…"

"A sucker is born every minute."

JOHN R. "JACK" CASSADY

"Ever have days when you just don't feel Gothic?"

"Looks like the music teacher checked out
everything on the accordion."

"I'm getting a text message from the other side."

"Knock off the rain dance. We're getting reports of acid rain."

"Fire drill! Everybody overboard!"

"I'm exhausted, I spent all day chipping
coupons!"

"Hold off serving the souffle'. Bernie can't find
his hat."

CHAPTER 2.

CHILDHOOD MEMORIES...
(Anecdotes from the formative years...)

"A clear conscience is usually the
sign of a bad memory."

Author unknown

She Put a Spell on Me or How I Became a Cartoonist...

The first new thing I learned in school was the concept of solitary confinement.

I could hear the laughter and voices of the kids playing together on the other side of the thick wooden door at the pre-school. I tried again to open it, but it was still locked and wouldn't budge. I relished the idea of joining the kids to play and make friends.

At home, a small apartment on the second floor apartment house in a middle class neighborhood, there were few kids my age around. I was about five years old and an only child. I lived with my working Mother. My Father, a Marine, was fighting WWII in the Pacific. I spent much time alone.

I remember being apprehensive when Mother announced she had arranged for me to go to a church pre-school program while she worked. She convinced me to go by saying there would be "other kids for me to play with and new things I could learn". It would be fun.

I was very nervous the first day she dropped me off at the pre-school. I must've been a late addition to the class because the other children were already there and as organized as a bunch of five year olds could be.

Mother told me to have a good time, and she'd be back to pick me up after work. I wanted to join the other children but felt like an "outsider". I was the only one wearing eyeglasses, and I didn't know what to do or how to socialize.

The teacher was a tall, stern looking woman dressed in black who reminded me of the bad witch from the *Wizard of Oz*. I'm not sure if she didn't know what to do with me or just disliked me.

Soon I found myself locked inside a tiny bathroom with a small chair, a short pencil, and paper. I didn't lock *myself* in there. I was locked up.

Solitary confinement is defined as "confinement of a prisoner in isolation from all other prisoners, often in a dungeon-like cell: a form of extra punishment for misconduct". I don't remember causing any problems requiring punishment. I don't think I had the chance; although, I might've said something to her about her appearance.

I do remember spending day after day alone in the bathroom. That convinced me the black clad teacher was capable of casting spells and other witch-like conduct. It made her even more terrifying to me.

The room was painted white and fairly bright due to a high unreachable window. I was allowed to come out for a short while at lunchtime to eat my sack lunch. Since I didn't know the other children and was kept away from them, their ideas of me as an "outsider" were reinforced. It was an unpleasant feeling for me.

After lunch I was escorted back to the small room by the teacher in black. As long as I had a pencil and paper, I occupied myself by drawing, much like when I was home alone. Drawing was my escape. I loved to draw and created my own worlds through primitive comics and comic strips. It was early Sequential Art and occupied my time and mind.

I'm sure Mother asked me about "school" each day, but, my communication skills weren't convincing. I didn't know how to verbally express how much I disliked school, feared the teacher or why. Mother knew how happy I was each day to leave school. Returning to the safety and comfort of our apartment was welcome relief for me. I suspect my Mother thought my dislike for school was normal, and I'd eventually adjust.

I didn't adjust; instead the fear and negative feelings grew. Eventually they manifested themselves physically. Each morning as I dressed for school, I became ill with severe stomach and headaches. It became progressively worse until my sickness was accompanied by vomiting.

The last day I attended the pre-school I threw up on the black clad teacher's shoes. Mother never took me back. I think that was the day the teacher put a spell on me. Rather than turn me into a small animal or reptile, she turned me into a cartoonist. Looking back, it could've been worse…

Salad…

Most children are chided to eat their greens. It was a custom at our house to eat a head of iceberg lettuce with the dinner meal, and I liked it.

Each person had his or her own head of lettuce which Mother washed carefully in the clothes washer. I always enjoyed it and never had to be chastised to "eat your salad!"

I found out that by punching the head of lettuce hard at the stalk, you could easily pull out the core. I really looked forward to that, since the core tasted sweet and could be used for dessert or a snack later.

The Hamster Fights…

Mother used to sew small trunks and boxing gloves for our hamsters. She called their cage "the gym" and every Wednesday night after church; all the kids would come over to watch "**the Wednesday Night Hamster Fights**".

It was very popular in our neighborhood.

Mother said the promoter, Don King was interested in our Hamster Fights but he never called.

I had to clean the gym.

Christmas in Daytona…

Growing up in Daytona Beach, Florida, I distinctly remember Christmas. There wasn't enough money for fancy presents, so most of the time I'd just get a big cardboard box – which is what most imaginative children end up playing with after Christmas morning, anyway. If the boxes were big enough, you could cut out windows and doors and pretend they were nearly anything.

Once I got a really nice refrigerator box. It was large enough for me to draw a number on the side and pretend it was a race car on NASCAR's famous beach course.

My friends and I dragged the "racecar" to the nearest grassy hill. We had a fine time racing down the hill until the police broke up our event. I think I was cited for "racing a box without a license…"

Grandpa Raced Motorcycles...

Growing up in a racing community, I used to enjoy watching my Grandfather race motorcycles at Daytona Beach, Florida. He liked to race on the quarter mile flat tracks surrounding stadiums.

He loved the speed and competition, but as he grew older, he was physically unable to continue the dangerous and demanding sport. He yearned for the feeling of speed and wind in his face.

When cars came out with sun roofs, Grandpa was one of the first to buy one. He'd let someone else drive fast while he stood up with the sun roof open, so he could feel the wind. People in Volusia County got used to seeing Grandpa standing up in the car while it sped up and down the highways. Unfortunately, it came to an end early one evening while following a speeding pick-up truck.

The lid of a beer cooler blew off the truck and hit Grandpa in the head. It knocked him completely out of the car. We stopped and looked for Gramps in the weeds alongside of the highway, but we couldn't find him.

Several days later, he showed up at the house with an attractive bar maid on his arm smelling like booze. He stopped standing up with the sun roof open, but he still liked to drive fast...

A Flashlight and the Races...

Back in the 1950's in Daytona Beach, Florida, NASCAR was in its infant years. The stock-car races were very popular, especially in the South, and as kids, we loved the races and the excitement. The race drivers were larger-than-life sports heroes to us.

I went to school with a nephew of one of NASCAR's early greats, "Fireball" Roberts. I also delivered the daily newspaper to the founder of NASCAR. I met Bill France Sr. a number of times and knew his son Billy from my paperboy transactions. Mr. France was a tall fellow with a great smile who treated me kindly. But, he did frighten me once.

It was a cool day in February near the time for the classic Daytona Races. In those days the big "200 mile" race was conducted on the "Beach" course. It consisted of a large oval track about five miles south of town that covered 3.2 miles. Half of it was on the sand of the beach and the other half on the pavement of blocked off Highway A1A. The location made it difficult to keep people from sneaking into the track area without tickets. A large security force was hired to ensure everyone bought tickets.

Early one morning after delivering papers, I rode my bicycle back to the France house to look at a shiny new Chrysler 300 parked in their driveway. It was brightly painted with advertising slogans and racing numbers. I was like a humming bird attracted to a colorful flower. I parked my bike in nearby bushes and slowly walked around the car several times.

I had a flashlight and a rolled up paper in my pocket. I peered inside the car through the windows. I noted seat belts and a faint new car smell. While fooling around with the trunk handle, the trunk popped opened. It was large, roomy and inviting, so I climbed in and shut it. I became comfortable and drifted off to sleep. It was easy since every morning I got up at 4AM to pick up and prepare my newspapers for delivery.

At first I thought it was a dream. Then I remembered climbing into the trunk of Mr. France's Pace Car. It was very noisy and from the motion I felt we were moving quite fast. The sound, motion and smells made me feel queasy. I'd never been sea sick before, but in the darkness, the motion was quite upsetting. I started moaning loudly, so as to be heard over

JOHN R. "JACK" CASSADY

the noise of a car traveling nearly 100mph. Shortly after my loud and persistent moaning, the car came to an abrupt stop.

Mr. France had heard a strange sound coming from the rear of the car and had stopped in the pit area to have a crew of mechanics determine the source. I didn't know we were in the pit area or that the big race had begun. Suddenly, I was blinded by bright sunlight as the trunk lid was opened. Mr. France was surprised to see me and he wasn't smiling. He thought I was trying to sneak in to the big race.

I quickly explained I was just reading my paper with my flashlight and fell asleep. I don't think he believed me. Nevertheless, he let me stay and watch the race from the pit area. I guess Mr. France enjoyed my story. Even for an adventurous kid, it was more excitement than I'd bargained for…

Cousin Barbara,

When we were kids, my cousin, Barbara fainted every time we had our pictures taken. She says she's allergic to digital photography. I don't think she's right because when we were kids, we didn't have digital cameras. They used old, analogue Brownie Box cameras. I think the flash caused her allergy. I hope she listed it on her medical records.

Uncle Millard…

My Uncle was a musically talented organizer and a really big guy. I remember the time he organized and choreographed several lawn service companies into a precision drill musical dance team. It was way before the internet, "lawn chair drill teams" or drum lines.

These burley lawn service workers danced and played weed-whackers in perfect unison. Their machines presented a symphony of two-cycle engines and a cacophony of mechanical sounds and daring dance movements. Bob Fossee would've been proud…

Better Than a Rock Concert…

One of the saddest things about the 21st century is the demise of troops of organ grinders and their monkeys. As a small child I remember Mother taking me to see the monkey antics and to listen to the music of the organ grinder. To me it was better than a rock concert.

However, signaling my approval by waving a lit cigarette lighter tended to upset the monkey.

Then I'd have to explain to Mother where I got the cigarette lighter.

Union Influence?

The loss to our modern culture of organ grinders and their monkeys is immeasurable. My Uncle said big labor unions organized the monkeys, and the resulting excessive costs put the organ grinders out of business. I wonder if they could qualify for a government bailout.

The Yo-Yo guys...

I used to look forward to the Yo-Yo guys coming to town when I was a kid. These guys were amazing professionals. They could do the most fantastic Yo-Yo tricks imaginable.

They'd perform on stage at the movie theaters before the feature film and were sponsored by Yo-Yo manufacturers. After the show all the kids would hurry to buy a new Yo-Yo to practice the tricks seen. We thought if we bought the same brand of Yo-Yo used by the pros, we'd be able to do the tricks.

It's important to remember that the pro Yo-Yo guys would do tricks with both hands at the same time. I figured the only way to top them would be to learn to do the tricks with both hands and one foot at the same time. I knew if I practiced enough, I would be propelled to fame on the Yo-Yo circuit.

I acquired three Yo-Yos and began practicing at home. I hopped around our apartment for hours at a time, crashing into furniture, breaking things and generally creating mayhem.

One day my Yo-Yos disappeared. It was as if they'd vanished into thin air. Mom said she knew nothing about it, but I've always suspected she saved me from my dream.

The Tragic Yo-Yo Accident.

As "paperboys," our little group delivered the *Daytona Beach News Journal* newspaper and hung around together. We loved going to traveling Yo-Yo demonstrations put on by professionals, and we were pretty good with Yo-Yos. We quickly learned the secrets of "walking the dog", "rocking the baby" and others. We also loved showing off our skills to friends and families.

One December a group of us went to a demonstration by one of the Duncan Yo-Yo pros at a theater before the feature movie. It only cost the price of admission. So, seeing new Yo-Yo tricks, as well as a movie, was a good deal. We looked forward to seeing a **new "around the world" trick**. Most of us knew how to do the basic trick, but this was advertised as a "New and **Improved** around the World" trick. We were skeptical, but curiosity overcame us.

We sat in the front row closest to the stage. The Yo-Yo guy came out, made some remarks and began his impressive routine. The "New and Improved around the World" trick involved propelling **two Yo-Yos** with both hands at a very high speeds. Once at the end of the strings, the Yo-Yos were manipulated to circle the demonstrator **three times** before returning to the normal Yo-Yo routine. We knew how to do one rotation with one hand, but had never heard of doing three complete rotations with one hand, let alone **both** hands. We waited in anticipation as the Yo-Yo demonstrator Yo-Yoed faster and faster to the beat of funky Latin-American background music. The Yo-Yos were traveling so fast, they were just a blur when it happened.

One of the strings broke, and the Yo-Yo became a high velocity missile headed for our row.

I jumped out of the way just as the hard wood Yo-Yo hit my friend Henry squarely in the forehead with a sickening "thunk" sound. The impact snapped his head back and rendered him unconscious. The movie manager turned the lights up and after several minutes, revived Henry with free Coke and Popcorn. We stayed for the movie then went home.

Henry was never quite the same after that incident. None of us ever tried to master the "New and Improved Around the World" trick. Later Henry changed his name and went to Hollywood. He became a successful actor appearing in a number of movies and print commercials. None of them involved Yo-Yos.

CHAPTER 3.

KIDS DO THE DARNDEST THINGS...

(Cartoons inspired by children.)

"We never really grow up; we just
learn how to act in public."

Author unknown

"It's embarrassing when your phone is smarter than you are…"

"These child-restraint seats are great!"

JOHN R. "JACK" CASSADY

"You must have the wrong number. Our little boy would never skip school."

"Your son is the class clown."

JOHN R. "JACK" CASSADY

"Your Mother has asked me to talk to you about
your advertising."

"Something just doesn't look right…"

"Mom just cleaned the floor and furniture.
You'd better take off your shoes and pants."

"You'll never get **me** up
in one of those things."

"Must be a full moon tonight…"

"Chicken soup may be good for my cold, but it sure clogs up my water gun."

JOHN R. "JACK" CASSADY

"I <u>do</u> pay attention in class. I just remember the wrong stuff."

"He's an organic metronome."

"Your parents have been kidding you. This
'sick hamster' is a ball of under-the-bed fluff!"

"I already know about sex. Tell me about apps, downloads and the cloud!"

"If I don't have permanent teeth, why worry about cavities?"

"Don't you realize that <u>this</u> is really going to screw up my resume'?"

JOHN R. "JACK" CASSADY

"Stop telling everyone you were held hostage. I
made you stay after school for 15 minutes."

CHAPTER 4.

DOGS, CATS AND CRAZY CRITTERS...
(Animal inspired cartoons)

"We can judge the heart of a man according to his love for animals."

I. Kant

"I think we owe the children an apology."

"Have you seen my dentures?"

JOHN R. "JACK" CASSADY

"His trainer was a multi-tasker."

"Just because you were a military working dog, doesn't mean all the other dogs must salute you."

"Nothing's the same since he coughed up a blonde hair-ball…"

Pablo Picasso
Spanish Cubist
1881-1973
Cat: Raul

PABLO PICASSO'S CAT

Vincent Van Gogh
Dutch Post Impression Expressionist
1853-1890
Cat: Theo

Vincent Van Gogh's CAT

Henri Toulouse-Lautrec
French Impressionist
1864-1901
Cat: Guy

Salvador Dali
Spanish Surrealist
1904-1989
Cat: Galuchka

S. Dali's Cat

Andy Warhol
American Pop Artist
1928-1989
Cat: Campbell

ANDY WARHOL'S CAT

"Well, I didn't make any long distance calls to Pomerania."

Eye exam at the Canine Ophthalmologist's office…

JOHN R. "JACK" CASSADY

"Are you the mastermind behind this?"

JOHN R. "JACK" CASSADY

"How come we never fly south for the winter?"

"Stay in the shallow end!"

"…Birds ended up with feathers. That's why
you can't have a furry Godmother!"

"Gee, I never thought about it. What's yours---a crocodile or an alligator?"

"I'd like to talk to someone about my Twitter account…"

JOHN R. "JACK" CASSADY

"I've had special training in security, drug and bomb sniffing, chasing bad guys and playing dead."

"He's calls it his 'smart bone'…"

John R. "Jack" Cassady

"Never sit on anything that even looks like an egg after a hailstorm."

"It's a different crowd when you put out the 'wild bird' seed."

"You tossed and turned all winter..."

JOHN R. "JACK" CASSADY

CHAPTER 5.

HOLIDAY GAGS, CARDS AND EPILOGUE...

(A sampling of holiday humor from the Cassadys)

"The trouble with life is there is
no background music…"

Author unknown

Easter coming so close to **St. Patrick's Day** caused the Bunny unexpected problems...

Happy Easter!

The real meaning of Easter is worth more than all the Leprechaun's gold!

"It was bound to happen."

JOHN R. "JACK" CASSADY

Texting cat.

"The trouble with Trick or Treating is it's too seasonal."

"The trouble with Thanksgiving is that afterwards, we eat left over penguin for weeks."

HAPPY
THANKSGIVING

JOHN R. "JACK" CASSADY

Merry Christmas
&
Happy New Year

JOHN R. "JACK" CASSADY

May the Great Spirit
of Christmas show love
for us, and help us to know,
like the soaring eagle, the
heights of knowledge.
May we be filled by the
gifts of fortitude, generosity,
respect and wisdom, so that
we may help others walk
the path of understanding,
love, and peace in this season
and the next.

THE CASSADYS

TEXT INSPIRED BY A LAKOTA PRAYER

...Christmas at the Cassadys... ..

JOHN R. "JACK" CASSADY

Merry Christmas & Happy New Year!

from the Cassadys

An Irish Christmas Blessing

The light of the Christmas star to you

The warmth of home and hearth to you

The cheer and good will of friends to you

The hope of a childlike heart to you

The joy of a thousand angels to you

The love of the Son and God's peace to you

JOHN R. "JACK" CASSADY

"This year I'm giving all those I care
for dead birds."

CATS CATS CATS, HARPER & ROW, PUBLISHERS, N.Y.

JOHN R. "JACK" CASSADY

FROM THE AUTHOR

I sincerely hope you experienced as much joy, amusement and entertainment reading this book as I did illustrating and writing it.

Every drawing and anecdote was inspired by acquaintances, experiences, family, friends, pets and animals. If you look carefully, you may find yourself or someone you know in these pages.

I should also add a special thanks to the helpful team at Xlibris publishing and to those who can't talk for themselves, our furry family and friends over the years. Some of the O'Cassady Clan are: Bandit, Maggie, Daisy, Mattie, Valor Jack, Bo, Brendie, Blackie and Dusty, Charlie, Jenny, Princess, Duchess, Purry, Mickey, Sylvia, Sasha, Suki and Murphy.

A portion of any profits derived from the sale of this book will be donated to my favorite people and animal charities.

Keep smiling!

Jack Cassady www.ToonMaker.com

THIS JUST IN!

Shortly after release of this book an announcement was received from the Department of Homeland Security revealing the mysterious disappearance of Jack Cassady. It's strongly suspected he was abducted by aliens. However, at this time it is unknown if the aliens were illegal or from outer space. Nevertheless, as of this report, nobody has come forward to pay the $39.95 U.S. ransom demand.

Please go to
www.toonmaker.com/TheBestOfMondayFunniesandMore.shtml
for updates.

Edwards Brothers Malloy
Thorofare, NJ USA
April 8, 2013